Songlines In The Wilderness

A Poetry Collection

Jack Zaffos

Songlines In The Wilderness

Copyright © 2016 by Jack Zaffos

Published by Local Gems Press

www.localgemspoetrypress.com

I dedicate this book of poems to Linda, my loving wife and my daughter Laura. I dedicate this book also to the Long Island poetry community who welcomed me and encouraged me.

I dedicate this book also to Bob Svenson for his long time support, to Temple Sholom of Floral Park, N.Y and to the FCE New York Ongoing Community.

Foreword

I have been fortunate and am grateful. I have had the opportunity in my life to do work that I have loved. I have had the opportunity to do work that has been an expression of who I am and my values. I have supported, encouraged, and empowered. I have tried to develop the skill of listening, and nurture the qualities of empathy and compassion. I have done this through a career of Therapeutic Recreation and Intensive Case Management.

In June 2015, I fully retired and now my passion has become poetry. I've written since I was 18 while in my freshman year in college. I have written off and on. In May 2008, I retired from full time work and worked part time for the next seven years.

With the support and help from workshop leaders and support from the Long Island Writing and Poetry Community, and the Writer's Beit Midrash of Skirball Insitute, I began to learn further the art of writing poetry.

These poems are personal but I hope they are universal as well. I hope there is a familiar chord that strikes in you as you read these poems. We all have disappointments and we are broken and on some level we find ourselves in the wilderness. The wilderness is the place between, the reorienting, the emptiness. These poems are meant to be songlines in the wilderness. That is a familiar lyric, a familiar note, where you may say, that's it, I know that song, maybe I can go there.

The phrase Songlines In The Wilderness was a writer's prompt provided by a workshop leader from the Writer's Beit Midrash. She got this from Avivah Zornberg, a renown biblical commentator who used the phrase as a means to describe Miriam's role for the Hebrews in the wilderness in Exodus. Dr. Zornberg has graciously given me permission to use the phrase as this book's title. What came from that writing session in 2012 was the title poem of this book.

I knew then also that if I ever came out with a second book after Meditations Of The Heart it would be entitled Songlines In The Wilderness.

I sincerely hope that these poems can be Songlines In The Wilderness for your trek as well.

Jack Zaffos
February 1, 2016

Table of Contents

A Breath Of Song

Walking
Taking a breath
Moving through the wilderness
Tired, weary
With contention and doubt,
Not knowing what is true.

I breathe and sing a tone.
A song line from the wilderness.
G-d, may I sing it loud
For You.

Enlighten me
And may I know
The inner spark,
The inner spark
Of a light within.
So I will nurture it.
Set it for a miracle.

The wind blows!
I answer.
The wind blows
Sheets of rain in my face.

I answer with a breath
Of song
Melodic from my throat,
Answering the wet wind
That soaks me.

A Work In Progress

This is a work in progress.
Don't just assume
And judge what's there
Or what you think is there.

This is a work in progress.
Things grow, things decay
Hello Goodbye
The next moment, another surprise.

This is a work in progress.
So if you assume
You make an ass of "u and "me"
So sit back and wait and let it be.

This is a work in progress.
The end (if there is one) is not to be believed
So sit with the tension
And watch it unfold.

This is a work in progress.
Sunup
Sundown
Around and around.

It's Time to Open The Door

I peer out from this locked room,
a prisoner of old images
and tales told too many times.
I see the sky, the sun shining through the clouds.
The scene from a dream
from many years ago.
A dream reenacted again, again.
Yes this locked room is not the world
though I find I keep the doors locked.
I fear the outside.
Is it too overwhelming?
Yet I long for that sky with breast like clouds,
I've always known where I needed to be.
I do have the key,
I've had it all along.
It's time to open the door.

Trust and Faith

Images appear from past times.
Memories of affections, trust,
and shared intimacies
over these past years.

Hidden vulnerabilities,
concealed secrets
only shared when
trust and faith are found.

Over these long years
I have known wondrous souls
of wisdom and folly
who have yearned to give and receive.

I have known and I have given,
sometimes feeling the strain
where an inner limit is pressed upon.
But I have been blessed
by those I have known.

I can only wish
that this wonderment
does not end.

For if it does
a glow in the world
will have dimmed.

From a Pier On an Inlet by The Gulf Coast of Florida

Voices singing
Drums beating
Joyful sounds
From across still waters.

The gift of music
Rhythm sounds
And voices unfettered
Carried by river breezes.

Last Words (A Drabble)

I ponder as I see
What's around me,
The joys, the suffering
Losses and gains
Souls carrying on.
I see that
And ask
Who speaks the last words?

I remember two friends
Writing visionary works
Their capacities lost
To chemical changes in the brain.
Where do all these visions go?
I ask again
Who speaks the last words?

I am buoyed by acts of kindness.
My eyes moisten when I encounter integrity.
But all that could become a void
From floods of nature,
From floods of syndromes,
Time and finally death.
So I ask again
Who speaks the last words?

8

A Gift

An act of love
Remembered on a warm afternoon
As I remember a day of younger age.
An act of kindness,
Sensually gentle
And disarming
Inviting me to enter
A new realm of receiving
And being received.

Now I think back
To that day
And now I can realize
I entered a place
Of a gentle love.

Reflections On A walk

Such a short time.
Life condensed
into a reduced container
of memories.
I walk the meadow path
seeing the blue blue sky,
and I walk the snowy lane
on a cold starry night.
Now presently
life seems short.
I envision the themes the dreams,
they come back to me.
I miss the light,
I have the memories.

The songline returns again, again
like whispers in the air,
or a throbbing of the heart
or a calling of the Soul.

Raindrops fall into a heartspace
nurturing visions of grace.
Memories and the present moment
lead to paths and patterns

and now it all can be seen as One.

The One that smiles from a place within
and leads me outward to this connecting path
where self-love and love for others is ingrained
in feeling, thought and action
in action, thought and feeling.

I know that place of compassion and
have sailed on Her river,
and on occasion have sat and sipped tea with Her.

The Jewel

When the Jewel is abandoned
 the land cannot grow.
That sapphire star that glows in the vessels
 shedding the healing from a glowing splendor.

When the site of the Jewel is left for lost,
 Souls do wither and latch on to twine
 in a raging desperation.
Celebration is lost
 replaced by mask smiles
 of a weird cyber-joy.

I know,
 I have often left the jewel.
Left it for lost,
 hidden under a thought-fortress,
 in a box called pipe dreams,
 to allay the fears of wonder.

The Real Revolution (Songs From The Wilderness)

I hear songs from the wilderness
In a quiet café
Where the mind takes me
To uncharted places
That remind me of times
On a path of thistles
Of summer walks
And the hard frozen paths
Of the cold depths.

I hear songs from the wilderness
From old markers along the way
Not knowing if others can hear them
Not knowing if others can know them.

I hear again
The voice of an old acquaintance
An Irish woman activist,
Who said   *Ah Jack,*
You are looking for the real revolution.
And then she sighed.
I could not understand her at the time.

I still search for the open heart
I still search for the listening ear
I still search for the courageous soul
I still search for The Silent Pulse
Of the Real Revolution.

The Tear From the Eye of the Heart

I know the tear from the eye of the heart.
I've felt the heart that breaks,
I know the Souls that have traveled with me.
I know the peace,
I know the turmoil,
I know the aching place
just outside the empty center.
I hear the disclosures and
I speak my piece
as I'm standing raw and naked.

I know the tear from the eye of the heart
a heart with walls too high to climb over.
A heart so shaded it doubts all grace,
a heart not alone but lonely.

I know the tear from the eye of the heart.
I see the breaking,
the blind rage,
the cold cruelty,
and the pain of victims and refugees,
and the helpless wondering

What can we do?

I know the tear from the eye of the heart
from friends who share their essence
and those who I love, as I
long to find a satisfaction from a wholeness
and belonging.

I know the tear from the eye of the heart.
The tear that binds us close
with the vines of vulnerabilities
and the arms of celebration.
That goes with us on journeys to a barren desert
and stays with us when we enter succulent gardens.
The tear that melts hard husks
and maybe then we feel the graceful hand
of a Soul waking beside us.

A Prayer For Despair

The darkness hid the grace.

The force from the heart was forgotten.

The fear eclipsed the vision.

For awhile now the side of the road
has been shrouded by haze.

The thought storms blocked the sunshine
and the meadows became barren.

And the light became alien
and I began to hide and wonder
how fleeting is this glow
how transient is this connection
how trustworthy is the Holy.

There has always been doubts
but the doubts overtook.
And though I sang the Songline
it was often murmured
and it could not be heard.

I say a prayer to once again
open the lips, eyes and ears.

A Memory

It was summer.
There was a known breeze
off the shore.
The day so long
it went on and on.
Young boy sitin' at the picnic table
free and unfettered.
Today there was no care.
No care today for the boy whose life was hard.
Today life was easy.
Easy as the breeze,
easy as the background lilting tunes
of the late 1950's
as music played from the table
at the next tree.

The sun unhurriedly went down the summer sky
as the air did slowly cool
as the music went on and on.
This boy's life was hard getting on.
But today life was easy.
Oh so easy.

Dream Of A Word

Bring out the stars
in this cold night
by this vast seashore
I hear the ocean roar.

I am wandering
looking for what I have lost,
wounded, tired,
looking for a word.

Wandering on the sand
to the road by daybreak,
then walking on quiet streets,
I believe I have found the word
hiding in an old library.

I smile,
shake off the dust,
hold it carefully
in my hand.

This morning I am content.

Song Lines in The Wilderness

I hear the Song line, faintly at times
Dimly amidst the dissonance.
I hear that Song Line
Though not sure how to sing it.
It beckons
To improbable places.

I know when I hear it.
Yes, I know when I hear it.
That persistent sound
Bringing forth a smile
And the relaxing of boundaries.

I know the song line
It rings true.
It returns again
And again,
Yet so fleeting.

All I can do is prepare
For when the
Song is sung,
To hear clearly
And listen to the tones of the moment.

The Portal

I in a time uncertain
Not sure what to do
A gnawing dissatisfaction
Is my companion.

A portal I see
And a feeling that if I were to enter it
And not be afraid
I can be free.

A steady beam of light
Cutting through the mist
Shining through murky waters
Covered by the dark and cold.

I wrap my collar tight
As I hear the pounding fog horns
Vibrating the bones of my chest.

The Lighting Fire

I am wet with mist and tears
I am wet with the ocean's waves
I cannot lose
I will not lose.
This shining light flashing,
Illuminating salty air
I see it on the water's edge.
Yes, I still follow the lighting fire.

The View From The Window

When it is upon you, you will then know
it's not going to happen the way you planned.
No, it won't be your play.
Not your created script.
Not the drama that you carefully planned out.

It's not your dream
Not your wilderness
Not your splendor
And the bows that you take
are not for the role you planned to play,
but there may be applause none the less.

After the blustering winds
that blew away your minds scenario
 you might try the view from the window
where there is that tree that blooms
early in the Spring.
Where the seeds and buds burst
and grow into blossoms.
When you see that happening
then you know you can do,
what you must do,
for you and the ones that you love.

Spring Haiku

The sound of city birds
Sing amidst an urban rhythm
As trains hum along

Round rocks in the soil
Immerse in the streaming water
While the flowing creek laughs

Grass sprouts in the sun
Spring's warm breezes bathe the ground
Sights outside turn green

Bush swaying in breeze
Birds sing and fly in the sky
Trees ready to green

Still Spring night tonight
Touch of coolness in the air
Fragrance of new life

Tree branch bends up high
Majestic view from window
A radio sounds low

A grey sky brings rain
To wash away spring debris
The air is gentle

Startled by a Streaming Spring

We enter a turning point
And face life as it
We carry on
Incomplete
Pressured to present a completion
To impress
And get chosen

What we say and
What we do
Become at odds
As we strive for the correct

And then we're startled by a streaming spring
Under the soul
Which presents us with who we are

the silent sound

i knew when it started to unravel
when all the plans would turn to dust
the old ways i could no longer trust
the game was over
it's just not the same
the party line now seemed so lame
i can't go back from where i came

i'd enter a place just playing a role
as if going through some kind of act
with thoughts hounding me and asking
am i conducting myself with tact
let's put an end to this masquerading
and all this unnecessary perspirating
to go beyond this rattling ruse
where i can hear the quiet muse
and hear the ancient calling bell
ring round… and round…. and round
….and then
the murmuring silent sound

How Long Til The Tulips Grow

How long til the tulips grow
reaching tall with flaming color
warmed by the sunny sky
swaying in the spring wind
a time remembered
as a time of growing love,
when the door of the house opens
to a new day of long forgotten warmth
with green grass rippling in a breeze.

How long til the tulips glow
there is a longing to see them again
for there are limited springs
in ones lifetime.
Limited times to see
spring emerge from winter's grip,
to see delicate stems
come forth through the soil.

The ice does melt
The heart does warm,
I wait for that
I wait for that
How long til the tulips grow.

Full to The Brim

The fig tree doesn't bear fruit
i seemed to have plucked
the last sweet succulence
taking it to the limit
and now i gag on tasteless matter
i chew and chew
but there's no reason to swallow
i am full to the brim

Hey Hey September Blues

Hey Hey September blues
Air thick with pollen stream
Clouded with unseen specks,
Sun on an angle
But it seems so bright
In the heat of a listless day.

Yes the day is shorter
But the heat seems hotter
It feels like the end of something.
The lethargic daze
From the pollinated haze
Somehow afflicts the spirit.

Emotions thicken
Like a muddy stream
Where spirit legs have to struggle
To move from heart to heart
As if going to places so far away.

Hey Hey September blues
The bright light blue sky
Wanes now
To a time of darkness coming.

Summer days are finished.
Fruits ripened
Are harvested or fallen.
Rays of sun glitter off the leaves
That are soon to fall.

Warm breaths of the Earth
Will soon be cooled by new breezes
That remind and remind
That the prime is past
And time moves on to another year.

Community of Loving Witness

Alone in a field
with a fear not faced
a terror not known
an uneasiness not shaken.

In a place kept unknown,
a desert where forgiveness
is wanted like a cold canteen
of cool waters.

Where one longs for connection
in a green meadow
up the rocky path
that leads to the slope
to the community of loving-witness.

Loving-witness
where understanding can enter
the vibrant stream
flowing down the steep slope
not seen yet from this present place
but known from a present hope.

The Last Room

This is not the last room
Though you may dwell within its walls
For a long time
Waiting there
And wallowing.

The walls around you
Surround the space you're in
Seemingly blocking the open air.

I say to you
It's not the last room
There are spaces so vast
So succulently green
That you have visited in your dreams.

That you have lived in your wakefulness
When you have forgotten these walls
And moved through the spaces
As a phoenix flies over the fields.

Remember this voice
When you are stuck in the pit of desolation,
In the cell of separation

Because the room of these walls
Created by the constructs of the mind
Is not the last room,
And you will cross the threshold
And leave this fleeting house.

I Ask Myself

The green tree brings me to the direction
of the moment.
Yet all kinds of titillation draws me away
into a private world.
Is this the condition of the human being,
I don't have a clue.

Yet I must ask the question
about the deep suffering of the soul.
Do I have a heart that opens
or a door that closes back into a closed room.

I ask myself
I am asked
We are asked.

Do I have hands that hold
or fists that clinch.

I ask myself
I am asked
We are all asked.

Oh What a Coincidence

Dust speaks and drums beat
blowing through the mind
through portals of weariness
telling me there's nothing to craft
but what a coincidence
I'm sitting here composing
through the shroud
called the block of the writer.

It is said by some
This is frivolous
Do some service,
something tangible
the block gets built
brick by brick
but what a coincidence
a bird sings by the window
a muse with feathers,
a throat and a song,
what a coincidence,
there's even more.

Songlines In The Wilderness

They sing from trees,
a sweet sweet shrill
sounding through the pores
of cinderblocks
used to construct these walls.

Painting a Snowstorm

Rapid flakes fall to the ground
Pinching the skin
With a sharp icy touch
While snow blankets the ground
As icy droplets
In a crystal swirl
Fly in a glorious wind

Reflecting droplets
Settle on a beard and clothing
As the fierce mist
In a crystal swirl
Fly in a glorious wind

The fierce misty cold blows
It is cold and dark tonight
It is cold and dark tonight
I sit with pen and paper
Spying snowflakes from a window
Spying snowflakes from a window
With pen and paper
Trying to paint a snowstorm with words

Michael

Michael was missing.
I received a phone call
From his old friend
The belly dancer
One night.

She said *Where he was*
No one knew.

When he was found
We found him missing
A patient at Rockland Psych.

I spoke with him on the phone
About his new kind of world.
Soon after he died
Of a massive attack of the heart.

A phone call came
From the dancer again
At first the news uncertain
She called me again
The news confirmed.

Twenty years earlier,
He called himself *Ty Hale*
An alter ego he created.
We walked the West Side
On balmy spring days
On warm summer nights.
We talked
We wrote
We read
We laughed.
And in the background
The white noise
Of Damrosch Fountain
Outside Lincoln Center.

We sat in all night diners
With strong coffee, and cantaloupe
And the poems we wrote and read.
Those were lovely nights
I still have a photo.

It is hard to believe
That I don't think of him day to day
But my path was so much changed
The evening I met him in 74.

I go to places
To visit old memories
But people,
This friend will not be seen
Unless at the *Olam HaBa Diner**
With coffee, cantaloupe,
A notebook and a poem.

- Olam HaBa is a Hebrew name for the afterlife, it literally means *The world to come*

The Parisian Coffee Shop (Michael II)

Hey Michael,
I have a book of poems out,
Just published.
I place the book down
With its violet shaded glossy cover
As I prepare to read the menu
At the same table
At that same coffee shop
In Manhattan, called *The Parisian*
Where we shared poetry
Many years ago when you were alive.
You probably wouldn't approve of the book.
When we read back then,
We rode an undercurrent of rivalry,
But there was never need for envy
For the house of poetry
Has many rooms.

Back when
We walked the streets of New York,
We told stories, joked and laughed,
And once got a warning from a security guard
From his loudspeaker, like a voice from the abyss
Saying ***Hey, Get away from there***

When we play acted mock pick up lines
With two mannequins in front of a women's
clothing store.

The city has changed a lot.
The Parisian Coffee shop though
Is still here in Manhattan waiting for us,
But you are not here anymore!

The people we knew are turning grey
And now there are vibrant young souls
Who now frequent our *hangout*.
I am happy they are here,
As the same waiters
A bit older
Wait tables
At the same booths
Where we wanted to remake the world.

Nagle An Avenue in Upper Manhattan

Colonel Cragel while eating a bagel
Attempted to finagle
John Livingston Seagell
While standing
On Nagle
An Avenue in Upper Manhattan

He met a shmagegi
Eating an eggy
And because of his diet
He was so leggy
Cragel concocted a drink
Called cream of the eggy
An egg cream invented
On Nagle
An Avenue in Upper Manhattan

Cragel met Ferkunkel
A long lost uncle
Who let out a cackle
When he saw all that spackle
But they saw it was Day-Glo
And they both went for Cocoa
On Nagle
An Avenue in Upper Manhattan

Five Minutes

It was only five minutes
Though it seemed so long
Entering the realm
Of being known,
By a soul met for the first time
Who spoke a short phrase
And gave a knowing glance
Bringing forth a feeling
Of being deeply seen
That rose to the surface
In blushes of embarrassment... and joy.

Time and tension leave the room
Replaced by the easy flow
Of conversations of the Heart
And understandings of the Soul.

There's a joy of being known and met
And the joy of a new companion
Next morning's journey won't be so alone
But with someone new beside me.

More or Less

It's been good more or less,
I've seen things in my life
and it never ceases to amaze me
that when I know a person,
it is so different from the first impression.
So much for the contention
First impressions say so much.

Because more or less
You can't tell a book by it's cover.
You can't tell the real by the concept.
Who we are is so much more
and it is wonderful when we are received.

For The Woman of The Wall (in Jerusalem)

White and Indigo garden
Drifting in the wind
In a vortex
On Holy Ground,
As the sunset air
Touches lightly on this Wailing Wall
In a unison
Set for millennia

White and Indigo garden
Joining in this Holy Pulse
A dance of devotion
Though sanctioned only
For half of the holy

Then what was Holy
Suddenly erupts
In sirens of rage
Cutting down swaying flowers
With the horrific machete of intransigence

Yet this White and Indigo garden
Returns from the Earth
Again entering the Holy Vortex

Joining again in ancient communion
With the Spirit of *Emet*
That forever renews

The Letter

Please bring us a little solace,
A little rest from the struggle,
A little ray through the window,
A little hope through despair,
Some compassion in the rigor,
Some freedom to the entwined,
Some strength to the weary,
Some grace in the harshness,
Some sustenance in the desert,
A marker on a trail,
A light in the sky,
A word on the heart.

Please bring us
Relaxation in the tension,
A voice in the silence,
Some silence from the noise.

Please bring us the poet's word,
The songwriter's song,
The painter's hue,
The actor's line.

Please bring us

Ears that hear
Ears that listen,
And tongues of integrity.

Please bring us
Waters that flow
Grass that grows
And trees that sway,
Birds that sing.

Please bring us the will to end hunger,
The will to end war,
The will to end prejudice and hate......
And may be this be Your Will,

Sincerely   A Human Soul.

It Is Upon Us

It is upon us
to open up
to what is around us
and look again
beyond the clouds of contention.

It is upon us
to find the spark
of splendor
ever present in the every day.

It is upon us
to listen......
Listen again
to the stream of life
within you
and the person beside you.

It is upon us
to find our fire
and flame it forward
to kindle the candles of community.

It is upon us
to look beyond
self made walls
to make our contribution to peace.

It is upon us
to study justice
pursue it
and speak it to power.

There is no edict
 over our heads
or a shackling command
that binds us.
We have free will.

But there is cause and effect
and we all leave our mark.
Reality's chain will have another link.
In the end will the chain be strong
or will we crumble from our own weight.

Witness and Wait

One more year
And the breath is breathing
And rivers flow through fields of grass
Fed by mountain rains
As they flow to the roaring ocean
Ceaseless,
All in a moment in time.

As birds sing
The Holy One weeps
For the hungry soul
The hurting rage
The destructive pulse of
The human shadow.

The Holy One weeps for the hardened heart
The jumping judging mind
With the rapid answer.

Life waits,
The grass sways,
The mist visits nightly.
The water flows,
The birds sing,
They all witness and wait.

What's Your Pleasure?

What's your pleasure dancing thoughts?
Moving as dream images.
Fantasies and fleeting adrenal rushes,
Thought dreams
That course through flesh,
Thoughts that seem so real
Engaging the taste buds
Sending the blood of embarrassment
To the head from a recollection of a social foible,
Sending a glow through the soul
From a memory of a loving encounter.
What's your pleasure my dancing thoughts?
Dancing round about
Creating a smile
Or a grimace from a perceived injustice
Or a tightening from fear.
On and on it goes
And I hope to sit
And whisper kindly to it all
What's your pleasure?

Unfinished

It wasn't finished, all that we need to say.
Something wasn't said.
It's just not complete.
The good bye was just too routine.
Like a passing **Have a good day**
complete with a social smile.

But behind that guise, I know it's not complete
because the memories flow on like an underground stream
and the reveries and dreams appear uninvited.
Yet we walk past each other with a wave and quick smile
as if nothing really happened.

What is it?

What is it
You rang my bell
You called my cell

You've summoned me
What is it you thought
What ways are we caught

You have my attention,
I'm now facing you
It is you I'm talking to

You want me to speak louder
I speak from the soul
I'm not playing a role

I'm tired of roles
I just want to be
What you get is what you see

Here I am in your sight
I want to be your friend
This isn't pretend

So what is it
I did hear your call
And I will give it all

All I Can Do

Clouds billowing
Gliding across
Sailing
Up in the sky.

Shedding showers
To unknown places
Like angels seafaring
In high air.

The sun goes down
Shining deep red
Surrounding these clouds above.

On the ground I sit
Witnessing this splendor
A particle in this endless cycle.

All I can do
Is hold my hand out
To fellow souls traveling in this rain.

Angels Go Rushing In

Angels go rushing in
to the point of creation,
to the original void
that no soul knows of
though destined to face.
To an unknown point
beyond striving and status,
and ideas and concepts
that carry us through.

Angels go rushing in.
We don't see it
lost in a fog
that passes for the real.

Angels go rushing in
to a realm
invisible,
immeasurable
by a gauging tool.

Angels go rushing in
to a void
that counters the excess.

To a simplicity
completing complexity.

Angels go rushing in
to an abyss,
an unknown,
where our very survival hangs.

We walk vulnerable
seeking purpose
or a Holy Place
not truly named
though ever present
as close as the breath.

Why Do We Shake The Lulav?

She forgot
the answer,
She even forgot
the questions
waiting there
to be uncovered.

This question revealing
like a gentle ray of sun
shining through a rain drop
that reveals the rainbow
from a white light.

The answers, questions,
the rainbow angel light shines
all around left right
front back up down
all around
Ever-present Ever-present

He forgot the question.
He hasn't asked it for a while.
That inquiry eclipsed by a cloud
that does not produce rain,

it just covers the light.

That cloud too familiar.
That cloud from the mind.
That cloud waiting to be
dispersed once again
by a Breath from a clear Vessel.

Ark Of Remembrance

In memory of Jonathan Cassidy President of The Little Synagogue

Holy Ark of remembrance
Crafted with love and devotion,
Within these fibers of wood
A Spirit dwells,
A meditative Spirit
Caressing the Holy Torah.

A great gentle soul
Has left us shocked and saddened
Yet somehow present
Within these grains of wood.

With loving hands
This ark was built
With a loving spirit
A community built
With a loving voice he spoke to us
Of dreams and stories
And with a loving passion
He acted for justice.

From his hands a wooden ark was built
To house the Holy Torah.
From his heart and voice
A spirit was built
To house the Holy Torah.

Remembrance

(Originally appeared as introduction to Book of Remembrance, Temple Sholom of Floral Park)

Memories visit us in the quiet night
when nothing is heard but a quiet hum
or a tree branch rustling.
Close ones come to visit from the days past.
We reach out but they are no longer there
for their physical presence is no longer.

We may no longer see a smile, hear a joke
or say **Thank you** face to face.
Yet we can say it to a presence
though no longer physical
can be as close as the lips.
And the jokes, the smiles and tears enter us
Again, again,
and again.
And again we remember.

Today To Let The Fire Glow

Thoughts so incessant
Boggle the mind
Take over the Soul
There is no space for the fire to glow.

Good things bad things
Harried things all things
Coming at me
There is no space for the fire to glow.

Mandated role demands
Logs pushed upon logs
With the sound of pounding collision
As they're piled so high
There is no space for the fire to glow.

At times I cannot see
Beyond this self made hill
Of should shouldn't and all that stuff
Though I know the light beyond that slope
The lantern light that sparks the glow
I breathe in open space beyond that mound
The mound of my making from the mud from my thoughts
Today I hope for space to grow
Space to let the fire glow.

In The Middle Lies The Window

In the middle lies the windows
of the senses.
The eyes, the ears, even the skin
will sense the window but not beyond it.
The glass, the tint, the smudge
and the creepy-crawly things
have called this window home.
We look through this,
we have no choice
but we can know the window
know the vision
and know the eyes that behold.

The eyes of silence.
The ears of stillness.
The skin receiving
and a soul that knows
and knows not.

And the window yields a little.
And the world sings anew
abound with smiles and songs,
berries and leaves.

Heard That Before

It's autumn once more
yet the trees are still green
below the blue sky
but the warmth will soon fade away.
The year moves on and we get set
for a new cycle in time.

The music plays on
in a suburban Starbucks
in a moment of time,
in a life time,
in eternity.

How does eternity speak
in this cycle endless.
Can we hear the whisper?
Beneath the continuous din
is the call softer than the quiet cricket,
soulful as the birdsong in the morning.

Yes the time moves
and everyone is moving
and when you get to a certain age
you swear you've seen all this before.

And the quiet call
beneath the sound of motion,
I know I've heard that before.

Remembered Wellness

No
Not any more
I won't carry these
Messages on my back
That serve me no good
That keep me down
And stifle the energies
That flow from the soul.

I won't carry this negative torch
Any more,
That keeps life force on the side of a road
And truth imbedded in a dusty nook.
This alien fire stifles words of Blessing.

I will not carry these lenses of confusion
Clouding sunlight and goodwill
And beauty
And the flowing grandeur
In the wind
That continues and continues
Seen when the bewildering lenses are removed.

I will not carry this cacophony
Chatting at the soul
Like some cackling ancient sound fury
Spouting, shouting screeching
Yet as I stop and pause
I lessen the soundings
And welcome quiet whispers.
Then I hear it all
I hear what is.

I will not carry the twine
That binds me
That prevents response
From a soft eye
Or an open ear
Or a heart of compassion.

No I need to carry on
What needs to be done
As I continue my walk in this world.

Only

Only the solace of the moment
receives the dawning conclusion
of the lifting mist
in the morning light.

Only the open eye sees the brightening sky
the open skin feels the zephyr
the open ear hears the spring that flows
underneath the rock barriers.

Rock barriers yield
only to the gentle touch of mist
held by the unknown presence
that holds the flowering bush.

Regulations Don't Care

(Or how to entertain yourself while listening to a finger wagging compliance consultant for 2 hours who inadvertently gave a writer's prompt)

Regulations they just don't care
They have no eyes or nose I fear
Don't know if I've seen a reg.
Walking or hobbling on a leg
Do they know anything of fear
Have they ever shed a tear
Do they walk down the hall like a zombie
Or do they whisper through a field like Bambi

But regulation they don't care
You can't go dancing in your underwear
So you better fret the consequences
Or you'll be talking like Senor Wences
You may say it's alright
But those around you will be uptight
Because as much as you may jeer
Regulations they just don't care

Walking Slowly

Walking Slowly
Wounded from surgical cuttings
On this one familiar street
Of pleasant memories
Acquired from walking on this path.

Speedily around me
Came this twenty something woman
With thin and well toned thighs
Covered by winter's tights
Running passed me
As a darting missile
As we entered the
Narrow part of the sidewalk.

Feelings?
Hey watch where ya goin,
Or
Hey life
I'll catch up with you when I'm better
Or
Has it come to this?
Or
What can I learn from this new found slowness?

Or
Am I getting old?
Lonely, as youth rushes by?

Perhaps accepting all of this.
I got to where I was going
To meet old friends
We smiled and hugged.

Feelings?
Feeling loved
Cared for
Part of something
Connected
These are feelings too,
They come and go.

How can we live with
Who we are at this moment
With acceptance
And self love.

Now I am the wounded slow walker,
That will change.

I was the darting twenty something once
Moving around past someone

On a narrow path.
Though harsh judgments towards this fast lady
Flooded my mind at first
They were quickly tempered by the irony of it all.

So I ask again
How can we live with
Who we are at this moment?
With acceptance
And self love.

What I didn't Tell You

What I didn't tell you
was who I really was.
I didn't show the scars,
you didn't see the other side.

The pain was hidden
and I showed you the niceness,
but I can be cold, I can be unmoved,
holding on to pride.

I've had my share of bleeding
I've had my pain,
The armors up
To send the heart below.

So please be patient
so all of me can safely enter,
the gruff, the fearful,
the loving-kindness.

So please be patient
as I enter out
and disclose a little more.

For in due time
I can assure you
you'll know my naked soul.

Next Month's Visit To An Old Friend

Time passes.
Days months years they carry on
as memories keep coming through.
Sometimes you meet a life saver.
One who can guide you to the center of your Soul
and lead you towards secrets of contentment and
confidence.

There are times when you are lucky
to meet the right kind of Soul
as if they were sent from a realm beyond
where Holy Messengers are born
who are sent to nurture blades of grass.
A realm I've glimpsed and where I've learned
to be a Human.

Visits to old friends are journeys to a sacred space,
when you know this could be the last time
and you know that this is when you'll know the true gift.

When The August Moon Rises

When the August moon rises
and the night air lightens
a breeze may blow from the cooling water.

A boat's motor hums in the distance,
from another direction a far away railroad whistle
and a breeze touches the skin.
You wish the moment would last forever.

The water endlessly drums on the shore.
The sound enters you
and connects with a deep longing.

You hear yourself sighing
as memories caress the soul
as the sea envelops the shore.

And the stars stand in the night sky
as distant as the furthest dream.
Yet somehow this vastness is
as close as the air around you.

As you are carried away by a singing sea
all thoughts go poetic

and take on the rhythm
of the pulse of the sea and the air,
and the silent psalms of the stars.

To The Lake One Day

I needed to go to the lake one day
The one with the soft waters rippling
In the wind the grass did sway
And I heard a sound so lilting

On the verdant high hills
In a breeze the branches were swaying
Not far was the seashore and the flying gulls
I even heard them baying

It was a placid place
Where memories arise
Away from the fast race
It's where the silence lies

I saw a reflection in the pool of water
Assure blue and a face getting older
Then from the hills I thought I heard another
Saying *please look again your spirit's getting bolder*

I was known by the evening

I was known by the evening,
by the chimes of the bells,
the summer breeze,
the eyes that gazed,
the mouth that smiled,
the colors of the wind,
the hum of the city,
the beat of existence.

I was known by the evening
by Tibetan Bells chiming,
the walkers on the road,
the fragrance of the night,
the caress of sounds,
the high clouds drifting.

I was known by the evening
by the music of the breath,
the Spirit of Souls,
the words of yearning,
the whispers in the wild,
the Source Of All Being.

This evening did indeed receive my offering.

Born To Poet

Born to poet,
For years I've always known it.

There were times to be discreet
But I never did retreat.

This legacy may not be great
But the Soul was written and it wasn't too late.

I cherish the wind, the branches the clouds,
The sun, the warmth and birdsongs not too loud.

I write the words, I write the lines,
And I find I enter the moment in time.

And the potential of the moment is also seen,
I pray to live on and see it green.

With flowers, trees and flowing grass,
And visions seen through a mind of clear glass.

About the Author

Jack Zaffos has been creating poetry since he was 18. Since his partial retirement in 2008 he has increased focus on his writing. Through classes and workshops, Jack is working on refining his work. He is retired from the New York State Office of Mental Health as a Therapeutic Recreation Specialist and an Intensive Case Manager.

After the last seven years of working as a part time Therapeutic Recreation Specialist, Case Manager and Researcher, Jack is totally retired and will be spending even more time on his writing.

He lives with his wife Linda and his daughter Laura.

Local Gems Poetry Press is a small Long Island based poetry press dedicated to spreading poetry through performance and the written word. Local Gems believes that poetry is the voice of the people, and as the sister organization of the Bards Initiative, believes that poetry can be used to make a difference.

www.localgemspoetrypress.com